PRAISE FOR

CW01494742

"As both a teacher and parent I was delighted when I read *CyberSense – the 7 Steps to Keeping Your Kids Safe Online.* As in his previous book, *The Con,* James Munton has combined attention-grabbing storytelling with easy-to-implement strategies for addressing the dangers he describes – cyberbullying, identity theft, the dangers of file sharing, password protection, sexting and more…this book is the perfect guide to give you the confidence you need to help children develop the habits that will make them responsible and safe citizens of cyberspace." –S. Burghardt

"*CyberSense* is a timely resource to help parents prevent online disasters from occurring, and to deal with problems as they arise. It's a great help for parents who want to do right by their kids, but need some guidance on how to do it." –J. Macnab, PhD

"What an eye opener! Every parent and grandparent should read this book…very valuable and practical ideas on guarding our children's safety online." –A. Long

"James Munton's message is directly on target for what our children are dealing with right now. I had the opportunity to see Mr. Munton speak at a conference recently and was thrilled to see his information in book form." –A. Bennett

"This book is hard to put down. I work professionally with children and families, and wish a resource like this had been written and available years ago." –K. Rettke, LICSW, LCSW-C

"CyberSense is a terrific resource as James not only talks about what can happen, but gives brilliant insight into taking a proactive approach to teach your children common sense safety in this age of technology." –T. Allard Anderson

"As a former law enforcement officer with 30 years experience, I was impressed with the contents of this book…I highly recommend this book to you as a parent." –G. Hester

"I read the whole book in one sitting. It really is a page-turner! As an educator and a parent, I recognize the enormous benefits of children having access to the Internet, but I also frequently see the trouble they can get into. CyberSense does a good job of describing the potential risks by providing fascinating stories of families who have had to confront difficult situations. It is ultimately a very empowering book, because it shares the simple steps we can all take to avoid these things happening to us." –H. Chang

"CyberSense is a concise and page-turning read which highlights online safety issues for kids and families in today's virtual world. This is a highly recommended read!" –C. Barberena

CYBERSENSE

THE 7 STEPS TO KEEPING YOUR KIDS SAFE ONLINE

JAMES MUNTON

Copyright © 2014 by James Munton

All rights reserved.

This book or any portion thereof may not be reproduced or
used in any manner whatsoever without the express written
permission of the publisher except for the use of brief
quotations in a book review.

Printed in the United States of America

First Printing, 2014

The Munton Group, LLC
PO Box 866533
Plano, TX 75086-6533

www.jamesmunton.com
www.cybersense-program.com

CONTENTS

INTRODUCTION

When I was a boy growing up in London, we had a rotary phone. It was heavy, and you could only take it as far as the cord would stretch, which wasn't far. If you called someone and he or she was on the phone, you would hear a busy signal, so you would have to dial and redial the number manually until the line was free. It was the same kind of phone my parents had grown up with, and their parents before them.

Today, my phone speaks to me. I can put it in my pocket. It's an all-in-one camera, calculator, computer, atlas, encyclopedia, address book, news station, and food critic. It can do just about anything but make me dinner, although I'm certain that day is not far off.

We are lucky to live in an age of innovation when technology advances so rapidly it makes our heads spin. Technology offers tremendous advantages. From research to communication to entertainment, technology has given us round-the-clock, instantaneous access. Our mobile devices are portable, convenient, and always at our fingertips. As with any new technology, however, there are downsides.

What makes life easier for us also makes life easier for those with bad intentions, people who use the virtual world to harass, prey upon, and otherwise target our kids. We hear the consequences of these actions in the news on a daily basis: cyberbullying suicides, inappropriate photos, sexting, child abductions, invasions of privacy, identity theft.

While we want our kids to enjoy the benefits of technology, we also want to shield them from the dangers. Yet we can't adopt a fortress mentality. The old advice is no longer relevant. It is impossible for us to police children 24 hours a day. Keeping the computer in an open area at home where you can monitor your kids' activity is equally outdated. Kids now have a variety of options for going online. They don't need to sit down at the family desktop any longer.

So how do we keep our kids safe? CyberSense.

The first cars appeared on the road at the turn of the 20th century, but it took another 50 years to develop a basic safety feature: seat belts. Seat belts were developed in the 1950s, but didn't become part of standard equipment in cars until the mid-1960s. Even then, they were widely ignored. Today, we take seat belt use for granted. When we get in a car, we instinctively reach for that strap.

My goal is for people to employ the same instincts when it comes to online safety. CyberSense is not about technical expertise or complicated software or jargon. It is about adopting a mindset. It is about knowing and understanding the potential hazards of online activity and learning simple, sensible strategies to reduce risk. Once our kids are educated and aware, protecting themselves will be just as instinctive as putting on a seat belt.

I have taken my CyberSense program to hundreds of schools across the country, helping kids, counselors, parents, and teachers recognize and avoid the dangers of the virtual world. Oftentimes I am asked if I have the information written down anywhere so it can be available even when I am not there. Now the answer is, yes!

The stories included in this book illustrate the risks of online activity in its various forms. Although they share elements with real life incidents, specific details, circumstances, characters, and names have been altered. They are meant to show what can and often does go wrong when young people do not use technology responsibly.

Technology is our friend, but as with any tool, we must learn to use it safely and wisely. As a parent, I am keenly aware of the need to keep kids safe online, but in order to be effective, we must approach the issue realistically and reasonably. Children are much more likely to act sensibly if they know why they should.

But before educating them, we have to educate ourselves.

What are the dangers and what can we do about them?

Read on.

1
PLAY NICE: BULLIES IN CYBERSPACE

"Ashley was always an energetic kid. I used to joke that even before she was born, she would keep me up all night kicking and moving around. As a toddler, she kept me on my toes. She was restless, always into everything, easily distracted. But I never thought too much of it, until she went to elementary school."

Erin is the mother of two. Her elder daughter Nina is a college sophomore who lives at home. Ashley is 15.

"In kindergarten, she often got into trouble for talking or getting up and walking around during class. Finally, her teacher suggested I take Ashley to the pediatrician to get her checked for attention deficit hyperactivity disorder (ADHD), which I did. Sure enough, she was diagnosed with ADHD, and the doctor prescribed medication. I don't know if Ashley fully understood what it meant. We talked about her

5

brain being like a roller coaster, going super fast, and how that sometimes made it hard to stop and focus on things. Although she was willing to take the medicine, she really didn't want anyone at school to find out about it."

Although it was not all smooth going, elementary school proceeded well enough, Erin remembers. The medication helped with Ashley's performance in school, and though there were the usual conflicts on the playground, nothing raised a red flag for her parents.

Erin was more concerned about what was going on at home.

"Nina, my older daughter, had no time for Ashley. Everything Ashley did annoyed her, and she made no secret of it. She made fun of Ashley, called her crazy, gave her a hard time about her medication and the ADHD. My husband and I did the best we could to stop the teasing, but I'm sure it went on behind our backs. Ashley would get so mad and frustrated."

Like many kids at her school, Ashley had access to the Internet at home via her parents' computer. When she moved to middle school, they bought her a cellphone. This is not unusual. A Pew Research Internet Project survey of teens and their parents found that 78 percent of kids aged 12 to 17 have cell phones. Of those, nearly half have smartphones.

"It was the school that encouraged us to get her the cell phone. They said it was a safety thing, in case she needed to get in touch with us or vice versa. They made it sound like she would be at a disadvantage if she didn't have one. So we got her an iPhone. And it did come in handy, if I needed to text and let her know I was on the way or if she had forgotten something at home."

From the start, middle school was more challenging for Ashley. It was a new school with new routines and an influx of new faces. Some of the kids she thought of as friends began to drift away and form friendships with other people. Erin noticed a change in her.

"Because of her ADHD, she had always been very talkative, sometimes too talkative. We had to remind her to let other people speak. But after she started sixth grade, she became more withdrawn, quieter. When I asked her about school, her answers were very brief. She didn't want to participate in any extracurricular activities. She spent hours alone in her room. I thought maybe if she didn't want to talk to me, she'd talk to her sister, so I asked Nina to approach her. They ended up having a huge fight. Nina walked out shouting, 'No wonder no one wants to be your friend. Look at you!' It was a disaster."

Erin relayed the story to a friend, who also had a child in middle school. "It was my friend who first brought up the possibility of bullying. She asked me if I ever checked Ashley's phone."

Because there is sometimes disagreement over what constitutes bullying, it's useful to take a look at its formal definition. As defined by stopbullying.gov, the federal government's anti-bullying site, bullying is "unwanted, aggressive behavior among school aged children that involves a real or perceived power imbalance. The behavior is repeated, or has the potential to be repeated, over time. Bullying includes actions such as making threats, spreading rumors, attacking someone physically or verbally, and excluding someone from a group on purpose."

Bullying is nothing new. It has always existed in one form or another, but advances in technology have taken the torment to a whole new level with cyberbullying. Cyberbullies use devices such as cell phones, computers, and tablets to bully others via electronic communications, including emails, texts, photos and online posts. Cyberbullying is relentless. While playground and classroom bullying is confined to school property, cyberbullying is pervasive, taking place 24/7 and following the kids everywhere. One victim said that she no longer felt safe in her own bedroom.

Previously, when kids had arguments in class, they were often forgotten by the next day. Now, conflicts continue and migrate online, where they fester and escalate. Technology has the ability to inflate disagreements exponentially, as messages are copied, pasted, and forwarded. Malice spreads like an infectious disease. While there is almost always a ringleader or two, the mob mentality takes over, and kids who may never consider bullying as individuals become caught up in what their peers are doing. For some perpetrators, cyberbullying is an extension of traditional bullying, but it also brings out the latent bully in kids who would never engage in bullying.

The anonymity and lack of personal interaction in the virtual world enable bullies to ratchet up the viciousness of their attacks. During in-person altercations, it is rare for a bully to egg on another kid to suicide. In cyberbullying, however, this is a recurring theme. Bullies are no longer satisfied with mocking appearance or rehashing arguments started in school. Online, they urge their victims to choose death, sometimes even suggesting the means.

When 12-year-old Florida student Rebecca Sedwick leapt to her death in 2013, it was reported that she had experienced prolonged bullying by a group of as many as 15 girls. The bullying took the form of derogatory texts and messages that urged Rebecca on to suicide. One text read, "Why can't u die?" Her tragic death made national headlines, but unfortunately it was not an isolated incident. In recent years, we have heard story after story of bullied teens taking their lives.

At first, Erin was shocked by her friend's suggestion. "I couldn't imagine that Ashley would keep something as serious as bullying from me. I had always told her she could come to me if anything was bothering her. But she had retreated into herself so much, I thought maybe she was keeping a secret."

Hopefully your child will alert you if cyberbullying or any other form of harassment is taking place, but don't rely on it. Be aware of changes in behavior and personality that may indicate problems. In addition to an increased likelihood of suicidal thoughts, cyberbullied students can experience worsening academic performance, emotional trauma, low or declining self-esteem, and depression. They may lose interest in school and social activities, exhibit physical illness, and have difficulty sleeping. They are more likely to become involved in substance abuse.

"The more I thought about it, the more I became convinced that my friend was right. But I wasn't sure how best to approach the situation. I didn't know whether I should try and talk to her first, or just sneak a look at her phone."

Erin had never spoken to her daughters about bullying. As a parent, you must be proactive. Don't wait for something to happen before you talk to your children. Engage them on the topic. Ask them if they or someone they know has experienced anything resembling cyberbullying. Ask them if they've ever participated in cyberbullying or ever said anything unkind about anyone online. The answer may surprise you. Discuss the importance of being accountable for what you say and do in cyberspace. Talk with them about which apps they use and for what purpose.

"My husband Mark and I discussed the situation. I thought that if I took a quick look at her phone, it would provide some insight into what, if anything, was happening. It would give us something to go on. We'd never read her messages before. He wasn't sure it was the right thing to do, but by that time, I was determined. I was on a mission."

Ashley kept her phone close by her side at all times, so Erin waited until she had gone to sleep, then went into her room to retrieve it. Sitting down in the living room with Mark, Erin began to explore her daughter's phone.

"She had downloaded a lot of apps. Most of them I didn't recognize. There was nothing in the phone's email program. It hadn't even been set up to receive messages. I clicked on the text messages and wham! It was like opening the floodgates. There were so many texts. I couldn't tell who was receiving or sending the messages, because there were no full names, just nicknames and abbreviations. I clicked on one of the names at random and started scrolling through."

Erin read with growing horror. The messages were like nothing she'd ever seen before, abusive and laden with profanity. "They were beyond insulting. They were obscene, almost sadistic. It was awful. The idea of Ashley seeing these messages, let alone receiving them, was unbearable. I felt sick to my stomach. I cried."

If cyberbullies target your child, take action immediately. Cut off the source. Together with your child, utilize privacy settings and blocking tools to keep the messages from coming in via email and text. Delete poisoned social networking accounts. Change email addresses and phone numbers. Notify the bully's service provider. If the bullying takes place on a social networking site, alert the site. Legitimate companies have policies in place to deal with threatening or harassing posts and messages. In 2013,

Facebook added a Bullying Prevention Hub to its site in an effort to combat bullying. Certain sites allow users to post anonymously, raising concerns that they facilitate cyberbullying. Encourage your kids to steer clear of these anonymous sites.

It's important to tell your child not to reply to bullying messages and texts. Do not respond to or engage with a bully. It is heartbreaking to read stories of suicides that recount how the young person spent hours online or on the phone checking and replying to hostile messages and reading the malicious things being said about her. Don't lose your kids down the rabbit hole of negativity.

Inform the school. The school counselor is a good place to start, but you may want to involve the principal as well. Some administrators may say that their hands are tied if the bullying is not taking place on school property, but cyberbullying is not an isolated phenomenon. If it is taking place online, there are almost always related incidents at school. For most cyberbullying incidents, a meeting with school administrators and the parties involved will be enough to curb the harassment.

You can contact the police if the cyberbullying continues or involves a criminal activity such as stalking, threats, sending sexually explicit photos or messages, or secretly filming/photographing someone in a private setting, such as a restroom. In one instance, an anonymous bully was using a third party website to send texts to a high school senior with special needs. The texts were violent and graphic and included references to rape. Although the website allowed the perpetrator to send texts with falsified phone numbers, initially masking the person's identity, police obtained a search warrant and were able to trace the user's IP address. They subsequently arrested the bully and charged her with harassment.

After reading through several text messages, Erin had to stop. "It was very upsetting. And the responses, pleading, begging for it to stop, they broke my heart. I just couldn't understand why she hadn't come to us for help. My husband took the phone from me and he looked at it. After a minute, he frowned and shook his head. I said, 'Who would do such a thing?' But it was almost like he hadn't heard me. When he finally made eye contact, I could tell there was something else, something worse. He showed me the phone and pointed to the messages. And I'll never forget. He said, 'She didn't receive these messages, Erin. She sent them.'"

Just as no one wants his or her child to be bullied, no one wants to be the parent of a bully. Erin's first reactions were typical: shock, denial, and disbelief. "Honestly, it was devastating. I couldn't believe it. Not my daughter. Never." She and Mark talked late into the night, agreeing to speak to Ashley together the following day.

Erin stayed awake the whole night. "Why? That was my biggest question. Why did she do it? Where did we go wrong?"

Some parents may have an inkling that their

children have bullying tendencies. Perhaps from an early age, their kids were the ones being aggressive on the playground. When confronted, they denied responsibility or pointed the finger at others. Some parents have bullying tendencies themselves. Sadly, those parents are more likely to go on the defensive when their children are identified as bullies and are less likely to try and provide helpful solutions.

For parents like Erin, however, news that your child is a bully can come as a complete surprise. And yet, like it or not, you bear significant responsibility for what your child does. You are the adult. Consider your own actions. Whether or not you realize it, you are constantly modeling behavior for your children. When you yell at a politician on TV or swear at another driver on the road, or talk negatively about friends and neighbors, you are setting an example. Kids are impressionable and they pay attention.

What is your attitude toward your child's online activities? Remember that social media sites have minimum age requirements. In the case of Facebook and Instagram, users must be at least 13 years old. Others, such as Yik Yak, set the minimum age at 17. If they do not meet the minimum age requirements, your children should not even be on these sites. Parents who allow their kids to set up accounts before they are old enough are setting a bad example. Don't break the rules and then expect your child to abide by them. Presumably you do not allow your underage children to drink alcohol or drive a car. Why would you allow them to flout the rules online?

If being a good citizen is not motivation enough, consider this: bullies get in trouble. School districts are taking an increasingly tough stand against cyberbullying and most have formal policies to deal with the issue. Punishments include detention, suspension, and expulsion.

Almost all states have laws in place to address bullying. In some cases, the laws are named for victims of cyberbullying who took their own lives. Depending on the circumstances, criminal charges may be filed. Authorities in Louisiana arrested a 17-year-old and charged him with criminal assistance to suicide after he bombarded a fellow student with more than 100 texts encouraging her to kill herself. The girl survived her first attempt at suicide, but went on to make a second, fatal attempt.

If your child is a cyberbully, there may also be legal ramifications for you. The parents of a Texas teen sued six of their daughter's classmates, along with their parents, for what they claimed was a pattern of harassment on the social media site Instagram. The lawsuit accused the students of libel and their parents of negligence.

Aside from these punitive actions, bullies do not fare well with their peers. It may appear that they have friends, but these "friendships" are usually based on negative, rather than positive, bonds. The characteristics most often associated with bullies do not make for good friendships: lack of empathy, aggressiveness, short temper, lack of respect for authority and rules, and a need to be in control. Do any of these traits sound familiar? If you observe bullying traits in your child, take a closer look at their online activity and nip any bullying activity in the bud. Kids who bully, like their victims, are at an increased risk of substance abuse. They are also more likely to become involved in criminal activity and be abusive as adults.

A child may not even think what he or she is doing qualifies as bullying. As an adult, it is up to you to ensure that your child understands what bullying looks and sounds like and knows that you will not tolerate it. Kids don't always think about the consequences of their actions. When they send something into the electronic world through a text or an email or a comment on the web, they may think the audience is limited to the recipient or a handful of people. But once that message is in the virtual world, it's out of their control, and they have to live with the repercussions.

After confronting Ashley, Mark and Erin realized that they needed to do more. They met several times with the school counselor. "She arranged for Ashley to sit down with the other girls, to make amends, and also worked with Ashley on constructive methods of dealing with her issues. It wasn't easy for anyone. But we had to confront it head-on. It was not just Ashley's crisis. It was a family crisis."

There is no way your child will get along with every one of his or her peers all the time. We have all been through the experience of having someone say something mean to us. And even the nicest, most amiable child is apt to say something unpleasant once in a while. But as parents, we want our kids to be considerate in language and intent. When we speak to someone face-to-face, there are opportunities to clarify, ask questions, gauge a speaker's tone, and engage in a dialogue. When texts are slinging back and forth, there are no such opportunities. Electronic communications are easily sent out into the world without thought or consideration. They are easily misunderstood and misinterpreted. While the original text may have been intended for the recipient only, it can be disseminated among and viewed by a large, unintended audience. Electronic messages can be viewed repeatedly and retained permanently.

If you have read the comments section on a YouTube video or a news story, you will be familiar with the kind of ugly remarks people post online. And these are adults, not children. Technology has made all of us less accountable and more anonymous, freeing up people to say things they would never consider saying in person.

In discussions with Ashley's school counselor, she brought up the fact that kids who bullied others online were twice as likely to be bullying victims themselves. Erin knew that Ashley had experienced teasing and exclusion because of behavior related to her ADHD. She also knew that Ashley had suffered years of verbal battering at home.

"We had to talk to Nina about the way she treated her sister. We had dismissed her behavior as the usual sibling rivalry, but it had reached a level of hostility and meanness that was unacceptable. Part of our plan to address the problem was to create a culture of kindness in our household. Be kind, not cruel. And if you can't say anything nice, don't say anything at all."

At the best of times, adolescence is an awkward period. At its worst, it can be torture. Bullies tend to prey on those they perceive as weak or having low self-esteem and kids who are different from the crowd in any respect (sexual orientation, appearance, background, disability, etc.). Kids don't have the sense of perspective that their parents do. Things we consider insignificant can carry great weight for them. Small slights cut deeply. Insults that we would laugh off can create permanent scars. It's easy to tell kids not to care about what someone says, but it's almost impossible for them not to care. School and their social circle define their lives. From emotions to brain development to self-esteem, teenagers are a work in progress. This makes them especially vulnerable to the ongoing nastiness that cyberbullies inflict.

According to a 2013 poll by The Associated Press-NORC Center for Public Affairs Research and MTV, 49 percent of those aged 14 through 24 said they experienced digital abuse, defined as any type of online bullying or harassment taking place through social networking, text messaging, or other technologies. The good news is that the study also found that more young people are turning to family for help, and that doing so usually improved their situation.

As parents, we need to be sure our children feel

comfortable coming to us with any concerns or issues they are facing, whether in or out of school. We also need to go to them, check in, ask about school and friends, ask specific questions about who they are hanging out and communicating with—not in an interrogatory way, but in an interested and caring way. Make a point of spending time with your child and his friends. If your kids are not of driving age, you are probably still chauffeuring them around. Listening to kids converse can be very instructive. They may even forget an adult is present.

Children today take mobile and virtual technology for granted. To them, talking online is as natural as talking on the phone or in person, and potentially more liberating. They feel free to say whatever they want to whomever they want. As our formal policies and guidelines catch up with technology, we are beginning to implement anti-bullying campaigns into our curricula, teaching kids what bullying is, how to prevent it, and how to deal with it. These efforts are essential, but they will have a greater impact if they are reinforced at home.

We must teach children and adolescents how to communicate civilly, to express their frustrations in a way that is constructive, not destructive; and to deal with conflict not through unrestrained ugliness, but thoughtful negotiation. The age-old lessons about playing nice on the playground apply online. If someone is being mean, walk away. If he or she continues to bother you, find someone else to play with. If there's still a problem, alert a teacher or other trusted adult.

There is no way to guarantee that your child will escape bullying, but there are many ways to stop the problem before it gets worse. Empower your children with the knowledge they need to recognize harassing behavior and the confidence to avoid engagement and to report it immediately.

A year after discovering the incriminating texts on Ashley's phone, Erin says the episode was a learning experience. "I don't take for granted that I know what's going on in my kid's head or in her life. If I want to know, I need to get involved. That's my job as a parent. And as difficult as it was, I think Ashley was relieved to have it all come out. She wants to be happy; she wants to be able to enjoy school and do the things an average teenager does. No one can be happy doing what she was doing. But she got caught up in something and didn't know how to get out. She's discovered what she should have known all along. Being nice makes for a better and easier life."

2
KEEP IT UNDER WRAPS: IDENTITY THEFT AND PRIVACY

Hayden considers himself a typical 13-year-old. He plays outfield on his baseball team and enjoys going on camping trips with his Boy Scout troop. He gets a weekly allowance in exchange for doing household chores such as setting the table and taking out the trash. He does his homework dutifully and for the most part gets along with his siblings. By all accounts, he is a good kid.

Imagine his parents' surprise, then, when the debt collectors started calling.

His father Bill relates the story. "We'd had calls like that before. We used to get wrong numbers so often that it became a family joke. But then one day, someone called asking for Hayden. I told the caller he must have the wrong information and hung up on him." But the calls continued. After a while, the family stopped answering the phone unless it was from a number they recognized.

"I finally had enough," Bill says. "I got the name of the company and looked them up on the web. I was starting to get suspicious, wondering if the calls were from someone trying to scam us. So I contacted the company myself. They told me that they were calling because Hayden had defaulted on an auto loan."

Bill was incredulous. "I tried explaining to them that Hayden wasn't even old enough to drive, much less apply for a car loan. But they had all his information—name, phone number, address, Social Security number. It was a very strange conversation. And it wasn't just any car. It was an Audi A6. So, you know, the kid's got good taste."

The agency representative, sympathetic to Bill's increasing frustration, told him that it appeared Hayden had been a victim of identity theft. She suggested that they obtain a copy of Hayden's credit report. "I've never even looked at my own credit report," Bill says.

Identity theft occurs when someone uses your personal identifying information without permission to commit fraud or other crimes. Identity thieves can set up new credit card, phone, and utility accounts using the names and personal information of their victims. They may also use existing accounts to pay for goods and services. Stolen identities are utilized to gain jobs, obtain loans, file fraudulent tax returns, forge documents, apply for government benefits, rent property, and do just about anything that requires a name, address, and Social Security number.

Finding the whole situation surreal, Bill and his wife Janine sat down at the computer and downloaded a copy of their son's credit report. What they found came as a shock. Hayden, age 13, with a grand total of $257 saved from his allowance and birthday money, had a credit report 20 pages long, with debts totaling over $75,000. In addition to the car loan, there were three open credit card accounts, all in delinquent status.

There is no way to confirm exactly how identity thieves obtained Hayden's Social Security number, but a common way to obtain personal information is to solicit it directly.

Although Hayden does not have his own individual device, he and his siblings have access to their father's old tablet, which they use to play games and surf the web. He is especially fond of word games, which he plays with friends and with his grandmother. Often while he's playing or after he's taken a turn, ads will appear, for TV shows or products. Once in a while, there will be pop-ups with enticements.

"I've seen ads for free downloads of songs, free cell phones, different sweepstakes, cash for completing a survey, things like that." And does he ever click on any of these ads? He does. "If they're giving away something good. I really want a Kindle or a Samsung Galaxy. Or an Xbox."

Hayden describes the process. Though they varied slightly, each ad took him to another site where he was prompted to provide personal information in order to be entered into a drawing. Though he does not know his Social Security number by heart, Hayden does know where his mother keeps his card, and was able to look it up. After submitting the completed form, he would usually receive a thank you screen and never hear anything more about it. They can never be absolutely certain how Hayden's Social Security number was compromised, but his parents believe that it was through one or all of these forms.

"I asked him how many he'd filled out," Bill says. "He guessed around eight or nine. There seemed to be some confusion about whether or not he was required to fill them out in order to continue playing. That disturbed me. Sometimes they were made to look like chat messages from friends, like, 'Hey, have you checked this out?'"

Bogus sweepstakes pop-ups are a form of *phishing*, a method of obtaining personal information under false pretenses. It takes place when someone receives an email or pop-up screen that claims to be from a legitimate source but is in reality fishing for information in order to commit identity theft. Both legitimate and shady companies use pop-up ads, making it difficult to distinguish between the two. A good rule of thumb is: when in doubt, don't fill it out. On the bright side, phishing is pretty easy to avoid by simply ignoring the bait.

I always tell people that less is more. As in, less information, more secure. Be stingy with personal information. Identity thieves thrive on personal data. The more they have, the easier it is for them to succeed.

It is important to realize that identifying information, especially a Social Security number, does not have to be provided every time it is requested. In filling out forms, we are accustomed to seeing blanks for Social Security numbers. Many people assume that because the space is there, they have to fill it in. This is not true. Certain entities, such as employers, banks, the IRS, require a Social Security number. A dentist's office, a grocery store, a utility company do not.

Utility companies routinely ask for Social Security numbers in order to complete credit checks for new account holders, but according to the Social Security Administration, this is not strictly necessary. They can use other methods to run credit checks. Before you give your child's number, you may want to ask why it is needed, how it will be used, what law mandates its provision, and what will happen if you do not provide it. Alternatively, simply leave that space blank and see what happens. The paperwork for a new patient at a doctor's office will always ask for a Social Security number, but if you leave it blank, chances are that no one will question it. I never provide my Social Security number or that of any family member while filling out these forms, and I've never had any problem.

Even when they're not specifically asked for it,

many people are happy to reveal personal information to total strangers. I can meet someone and within moments, know almost as much about him as I do my friends. Americans are comfortable broadcasting the most intimate details of their personal lives. We pour our hearts out on talk shows. We create blogs to share minute details of our daily routines. We post photos of what we're having for lunch.

The next time you're on your way to work or picking up your kids from school, take a look at the backs of other vehicles. You'll see bumper stickers advertising children's names, schools, and extracurricular activities, along with military affiliations, vacation destinations, and religious and political views.

It's no surprise that kids raised in this atmosphere are also free with their information. Having grown up with technology, born into a highly interconnected world, they do not harbor the same suspicions that their parents and grandparents do. Already prone to be less guarded and circumspect than most adults, they willingly fill in the blanks when prompted.

You can try to be vigilant and monitor all your kids' electronic communications and social media interactions, but parents can only do so much. Young people in the digital age are much harder to police. If you really want to protect your kids, you need to engage them in a discussion of online privacy. Teenagers are notoriously free with their personal information online. In 2012, the Pew Research Internet Project conducted a survey on teens, social media, and privacy, and the results are illuminating.

Among the key findings:

- 91% post a photo of themselves
- 71% post their school name
- 71% post the city or town where they live
- 53% post their email address
- 20% post their cell phone number

These numbers all represent an increase from the previous figures, released in 2006. It would be one thing if this information was only visible to a close circle of friends. But according to the same survey, the average teen has 300 Facebook friends and only 60 percent of teen Facebook users have set their profiles to private. This means that the other 40 percent make this information available to the entire viewing public. More than 60 percent of teens on Twitter say that their tweets are public.

When parents think about identity theft, they rarely think about their children. But they should. According to a study from the Carnegie Mellon CyLab, children are 51 times more likely to be the victims of identity theft than adults. Why? For one thing, as the Carnegie report stated, "A child's identity is a blank slate." Unlike adults, children have yet to incur debt. There's no paper trail of mortgages, car notes, student loans, and credit cards. Their records are pristine and ripe for pilfering.

Also attractive to crooks is the fact that the theft is more likely to go undetected for a longer period. Because they're not usually active in the adult world of finances and employment, minors have no reason to keep tabs on their credit history. Parents who might be diligent in monitoring their own accounts and records may never even think of doing the same for their kids.

Educate your kids about what identity theft is and how it works. More kids know how to play video games or operate computers than do things like ride a bike or swim. Being online is second nature to them. Chances are that they won't take the problem seriously at first. Tell a teenager that identity theft could affect his credit score and watch his eyes glaze over. Put it in terms they can understand. Scare them if you have to. Tell them that identity theft can lead to mistaken arrests. That they might not be able to get that scholarship they need because someone else is using their Social Security number. Tell them that information is as valuable as money. Would they leave a suitcase full of cash on the front lawn with a "Help yourself" sign on it?

We need to instill in our children a healthy dose of skepticism. Things are not always what they seem. People are not always who they say they are. It doesn't matter how legitimate a message looks, how authentic a person sounds, how genuine an opportunity seems. Verification is crucial. I say "healthy" because we don't want our kids to become completely cynical or paranoid, but we do want them to be sensible. Cybersensible.

Sarah, a high school junior, and her friend Kennedy found the perfect summer jobs as lifeguards at a public pool in their neighborhood. It would be the first job for both girls, and they were excited to apply together.

"After we put in our applications, they told us they'd have to run background checks. That was standard policy with all the lifeguards. Soon after that, Kennedy got a call to come down to the pool and start the training process. Meanwhile, I still hadn't heard anything."

Several days later, someone from the city's human resources department left a message asking Sarah to call back, preferably with a parent present. When Sarah and her mother returned the call, they were told that the background check showed that Sarah's Social Security number was in use by someone employed in another state, and had been for years. Until the situation was cleared up, the city could not offer Sarah a job.

Instead of working, Sarah, along with her parents, spent the summer trying to sort out the mess. "It was time consuming and annoying. There was lots of paperwork, filing reports and alerting different agencies. Basically I had to prove that I was me, and that this other person was the imposter, which seems ridiculous."

Unfortunately, not all cases of identity theft are preventable. There are instances where we do need to share children's personal information, and the information can then be exposed through malice or negligence. Schools, which employ large numbers of people and often lag technologically, are a prime example. Educational institutions account for a third of all data breaches in the United States. An early morning jogger running past an elementary school in California discovered that boxes of documents containing families' personal information had been thrown into a dumpster without being shredded. The documents included applications for free and reduced price meals. A North Carolina school system accidentally sent out 5,000 postcards with students' Social Security numbers printed on the front. Almost 50 percent of students have had grades posted by Social Security number. These types of data breaches are out of our control and while they do not always result in identity theft, they increase the likelihood of personal information getting into the wrong hands.

Because we can't stop every incident of identity theft, it's important to be informed and aware, and to act promptly once you detect a problem. Bill and Janine were alerted to identity theft when the collection phone calls started. If your child begins receiving mail usually reserved for adults, like credit card offers or correspondence from the IRS, that would be another red flag. Difficulties with any sort of application process, to access public benefits or gain employment or to receive a student loan, can also be a sign.

Credit monitoring is something that you can and should do for your children, as well as for yourself, at no cost. There are three major credit reporting agencies: Equifax, Experian, and TransUnion. By law, every individual is entitled to one free credit report from each agency every 12 months. By staggering your requests, you can view one report every four months. As former Equifax CEO Thomas Chapman said, "Relying on just one free credit report a year is like turning on your fire alarm only on weekends." Request a copy of your credit report, as well as those of your children, so you can monitor activity on any existing accounts and check for new, unauthorized accounts. To request the free credit reports online, visit https://www.annualcreditreport.com.

Before he ordered Hayden's credit report, Bill had never even seen his own. It was a learning experience for him too. After he and Janine reviewed their son's report on their own, they sat down with him to go over it. "I didn't want it to be a scary experience. We wanted him to understand that yes, this bad thing had happened, but there was a way to deal with it. As Janine pointed out, it was better that we discovered the problem while he was still 13, before he started applying for colleges and financial aid and all that. This way we could address the problem and stay on top of things." Hayden's parents also used the opportunity to explain why it was important to keep personal information private. He could see the consequences in black and white.

While prevention is always better than the cure, if identity theft does affect your child, do not despair. I suggest the following five-step plan:

1. Place a fraud alert on your credit report
2. Request copies of your credit report
3. File a police report

4. Contact the FTC
5. Document every step

Let's look at the five-step plan in more detail:

1. Place a Fraud Alert on Your Credit Report

Contact one of the three consumer reporting agencies to place a fraud alert on the credit report. A fraud alert informs creditors that they need to take added precautions before opening new accounts in your name or making changes to existing accounts. You only need to contact one of the companies, as they are legally required to contact the other two. However, you may want to follow up with the other two to ensure that they have been notified. Visit them online at:

- Equifax: www.equifax.com
- Experian: www.experian.com
- TransUnion: www.transunion.com

There are two kinds of fraud alerts, initial and extended. An *initial fraud alert* lasts for at least 90 days. An *extended alert* remains active for seven years. Unlike an initial alert, an extended alert requires potential creditors to contact you personally before issuing the credit. Be aware that fraud alerts, while important, do not stop identity thieves from charging purchases to existing accounts nor prevent them from opening accounts that do not require credit checks.

2. Request Copies of Your Credit Report

Once you place a fraud alert, you are able to request a free copy of your current credit report from all three agencies. This is in addition to the free annual copy available to everyone. Read through the credit reports carefully and look for any discrepancies or unfamiliar debts, loans, or accounts.

The report will also contain information on how many inquiries have been made into your credit. This will tell you how many times the credit file has been accessed by someone trying to set up accounts in your child's name. There may be credit inquiries even if no identity theft has taken place.

3. File a Police Report
Contact your local police department and file a police report. This report is known as an identity theft report, and having one will enable you to exercise your rights under the Fair Credit Reporting Act. It may be required by creditors in order to recover losses and will also be requested by the three credit reporting agencies if you are seeking to block fraudulent activity from appearing on your credit report. If you request an extended fraud alert on the credit report, you will have to provide an identity theft report filed with the local police or other law enforcement.

4. Contact the FTC
File a complaint with the Federal Trade Commission at www.ftccomplaintassistant.gov or by calling 1-877-ID-THEFT (438-4338). The more information the FTC has on identity theft and other forms of fraud, the better able it will be to help inform and protect consumers. The FTC will share the information with law enforcement agencies.

The FTC provides an identity theft affidavit form that can be used to notify financial institutions and creditors that you have been a victim of identity theft. The form should also be available through the police department.

5. Document Every Step

As soon as you suspect identity theft, start keeping a written record. If you confirm fraud, keep track of your actions. Whenever you contact someone by phone, take notes, get the individual's name, and log the date of the call. Send documents and letters via certified mail with a return receipt request. That way you have confirmation that they received the mail. Keep copies of any correspondence you send out or receive via hard copy or email. A careful record of all transactions and communications will help to keep the process running smoothly and will ensure that you have access to whatever documents you need at any time.

Identity theft is widespread, but its impact on kids 18 and under is difficult to measure because it goes largely undetected. There is no way to guarantee that it will never happen to your kids, but plenty of ways to curb risk by sharing with them the facts and the importance of keeping personal information confidential. You can also begin monitoring your children's credit history before problems arise so that you can take quick action if they do.

Hayden still plays word games with his grandmother, but his parents have disabled the pop-up advertising on all his games. He now views online offers with suspicion. "It's like the Trojan horse. It looks like someone's offering you a present, but really they're out to get you." He still covets a tablet of his own, but plans to get it the old-fashioned way, by saving up his allowance.

3
DON'T ENGAGE: AVOIDING ONLINE PREDATORS

Melanie is a big fan of meeting people online. After her divorce, she was reluctant to date, preferring to focus on her kids and tackling life as a single mother. But with friends urging her on, she finally decided to take the plunge and registered for an online dating service. It was, she says now, "one of the best decisions I've ever made." She met her second husband, Pete, within weeks, and a year later, they were married.

She's not alone. The Pew Research Center's Internet Project reports that one in ten Americans has used an online dating site or mobile dating app. And why not? The Internet is a valid and convenient place to meet people. Online dating, shopping, selling, chatting with people who share your hobbies, keeping in touch with new and old friends—these are all areas in which technology has benefited society immensely.

But with rewards come risks, especially for the youngest and most vulnerable among us. The key is to find a way to be aware of the risks without losing the benefits.

"I think I've done a good job teaching my kids to be responsible," says Melanie, who has three children ranging in age from 7 to 14. "At school they're always talking about making good choices, and I reinforce that at home. The divorce was hard on them, but their father and I have tried to maintain a good relationship. They see him regularly. It was probably hardest on Liam, my eldest. But they've all gotten to know and like Pete, and we've adjusted to our changing family life."

Like his mother, Liam finds the computer useful for communicating. When his father travels for work, or even when he is at home across town, he uses Skype to stay in touch with his kids. Liam is an avid gamer, although his mother limits the number of hours he is allowed to play.

"The gaming system is set up in our den, but those games can be loud, so I make him wear headphones," says Melanie. "I know he sometimes plays with friends online, and they chat back and forth."

One day Liam received a card in the mail with no return address. "He opened it, and there was a Visa gift card inside. I asked him who sent it. 'A friend,' he said. Which friend? I know all his friends. He told me, 'Jared.' Well, who the heck is Jared?"

Liam explained to his mother that Jared was a gaming friend, someone he had gotten to know while playing online. They'd never met, but they'd chatted plenty and spoken on the phone a couple of times. He was older, Liam wasn't sure exactly how old. Jared had asked for Liam's address and Liam had provided it without thinking twice.

"I was stunned," said Melanie. "How was this happening without my knowledge? Who was this guy? Why was he sending my kid a present and talking to him on the phone? Why did he have our address? My mind was all over the place. I asked Liam, why would you talk to a stranger and give him your address? He said, 'Mom, he's not a stranger. He's my friend.'"

When our kids start school, we educate them about stranger danger and how to avoid perilous situations when they're out in the world. This effort focuses on face-to-face encounters with strangers who might wish them harm, but does not include people they meet online or virtually.

During my school presentations, I make a point of asking kids if they play video and/or computer games with people they don't know. The number of kids who raise their hand always amazes me—and by the looks on their faces, the teachers are surprised as well. After playing online with someone several times, kids like Liam may not view the person as a stranger and may be willing to meet up. It is vital that the stranger danger message we taught them at a young age be applied to contacts they make online.

Online predators pose an immediate risk to children, who are affected through sexual abuse, abduction, human trafficking, and exploitation. As nightmarish as these possibilities are, we have to accept the fact that there are people in the world who prey on children. While there is no need to share graphic details with children, they need to know that it is as important to be cautious online as it is on the street. When your children are younger, take the time to sit with them while they're on the computer and go through some basic dos and don'ts. For example, don't use your real name as your login. Do let a parent know if a message pops up on the screen. Tell children that we don't talk to strangers online because we don't know who they are and can't tell if they're friendly or not. Some people may look or sound nice, but may only be pretending. Talking to kids about appropriate and inappropriate behavior will help them develop that gut instinct they'll need to steer clear of danger.

Technology has been a boon for sexual predators. Previously, they would need to phone the house, write a letter, or make contact in person. Now they can communicate instantaneously at all hours of the day without parents knowing. Technology allows them to pose as your children's peers. Researchers at Lancaster University in England conducted a study with 350 children and teenagers in which they found that four out of five kids couldn't tell when they were talking to an adult impersonating a child online. Predators will use text abbreviations and slang popular with kids. They can demonstrate empathy for whatever problems the kid's dealing with and will use any vulnerabilities they uncover to their advantage.

Technology offers a false sense of security. We think our children are protected because they're in the safety of their own home, but if someone with bad intentions has connected with them, it is only a matter of time before he tries to initiate more intimate contact. It also gives our kids a false sense of security because they feel they are removed from the person on the screen. Technology provides them with a buffer. It can feel fun and exciting, until it becomes all too real.

When Melanie discovered that Liam had started up a "friendship" with Jared, she was very concerned. "I tried not to get too upset, because I wanted Liam to feel like he could talk to me about the situation and not clam up. It came out in our conversation that Jared had told him he was going to come to one of Liam's soccer games. Soccer was one of the things they'd bonded over, apparently. When he told me that, I got a sick feeling in my stomach."

Here are some key points to share with your children:

- Do not engage in personal conversations with strangers online.
- Do not share personal information with strangers.
- If anyone you meet online, adult or child, asks to meet in person, tell a parent immediately.
- Do not post photos or videos of yourself publicly.

- Do not post personal identifying information on social networking sites.
- Use privacy settings to keep your online presence visible only to those you know and have approved.

Ask your kids this: would you open the front door and let a stranger inside your house? Hopefully the answer is no! Tell them that when they share personal information online, whether it's their name, address, or a photo, they are opening the door to a stranger. It's hard enough to tell the good guys from the bad guys in real life. Online, it's practically impossible.

These guidelines do not only apply to communications with strangers. Predators in your own community also use technology to communicate with kids. We've all seen news reports of a teacher or gymnastics coach or other person involved in youth-related activities being arrested for preying on children. If there is someone in your child's life who is taking what you think is an unusual interest in your child, who looks for reasons to be alone with children, who is texting or calling your child privately, you are right to be wary. It's common for kids targeted by predators to be silent when victimized, so you should be talking to your children about these issues and telling them to alert you if there's anyone who makes them feel uncomfortable.

The idea is not to give your kids nightmares, but to educate and prepare them. They need to know and understand the risks just as they know and understand the dangers of riding in a car. There is always the potential for a car accident, so we need to wear seat belts. Similarly, we have to use all the protections available to us online. Chief among these is being protective of our personal information and identities.

The more she learned, the more suspicious Melanie became. "When Liam told me about his soccer game, I had a terrible feeling that this Jared, or whatever his name was, had already been to a game, watching anonymously in the crowd. Liam said that they'd talked about going to a professional soccer match. The note with the gift card said that he could use it to buy a jersey."

As he told his mother, Liam did not consider Jared a stranger. After all, they'd spoken many times. Liam had shared a lot about his life, including the story of his parents' divorce. Jared said he too was the child of divorced parents. From what he told Liam, he lived in the area and worked full time.

"We had a very serious conversation about why it can be dangerous to form relationships with strangers and how he should never, ever, meet up with anyone he'd met online unless we'd given him permission and were with him. At first he just brushed it off, saying that Jared seemed like a cool guy and he didn't know why I was making such a big deal of it. So I went online. The National Center for Missing and Exploited Children has videos made by kids who survived encounters with online predators. I made him watch a couple. They didn't go into specifics of what had happened to them, but you could tell it was bad. After that, he got it. He understood. And he was scared, because he'd given this guy our address. He said, 'Mom, what if he turns up here?'"

Melanie told both Pete and her ex-husband what had happened and they all agreed that something had to be done, but what? Jared had not committed any crime that they knew of. Liam gave them the email address and cell number Jared had used to reach him. Melanie contacted the local police department and shared the story, along with copies of the text and email messages and Jared's information. Then, the parents worked together to craft an email to Jared.

"It was brief but firm. We said that we were Liam's parents and that he had told us everything. All his information was now in the hands of the police. If he ever tried to make contact with Liam in any form, we would go straight back to the police. We weren't going to move, but we changed Liam's phone number and email address so he would be harder to find. He changed his gaming ID and avatar. He even quit playing online. And we never heard anything more from Jared," Melanie says.

When I speak to parents about online safety, predators are one of their biggest concerns. How big a problem is it? Researchers at the University of New Hampshire's Crimes against Children Research Center carried out a national study on Internet-initiated sex crimes against minors. They discovered that 1 in 25 youths received an online sexual solicitation in which the solicitor tried to make offline contact. Of note was the finding that kids who engaged in four or more risky online behaviors were much more likely to report receiving online sexual solicitations. These behaviors included having strangers on their buddy lists, discussing sex online with people they didn't know, and being rude or nasty online. Sixty-seven percent of victims in the study were between the ages of 12 and 15. Significantly, the majority of victims had met the predator willingly.

Take the case of Delia, a 15-year-old who had a strained relationship with her parents. As a frequent visitor to chatrooms, she talked online with strangers regularly. One day, a user named Brian struck up a conversation with her that went on for more than an hour. The next time she logged on to the site, they found each other again and had another long chat. Eventually, Delia and Brian took their conversation outside the chatroom and began instant messaging one another, first daily, then several times a day. Even though Brian told Delia that he was 47, she found him easy to talk to, and considered him a friend. That friendship quickly became romantic in nature and he became the one person she relied on for comfort and support. Their conversations were the highlights of her day.

When Delia complained about her parents' treatment, Brian said he would never treat her that way, and that she deserved to be treated like a princess. When she vented about the behavior of her school friends, Brian dismissed them as childish and unworthy. Delia was way too mature and sophisticated to hang out with them. He made her feel good about herself. One night after six weeks of messaging back and forth, Delia told Brian she'd had a particularly bad day. "I just wish we could be together," she told him. "We can," he replied.

The Crimes against Children Research Center study showed that the majority of kids who met predators online willingly met with them in person, like Delia. This means that our approach to children cannot be limited to "just say no." Many of these teenagers are knowingly becoming involved with individuals who turn out to be predators. They just don't realize the potential consequences, how dangerous these people are, and how devastating the experience can be. They may have an idealized concept of a romantic suitor that could not be further from reality. They may seek excitement or escape from unhappy home situations or difficult personal circumstances. This person online seems to offer them everything they want and need. What they don't understand is that they're dealing with a predator, someone who not only doesn't care about them, but who will take advantage of and hurt them. That is the clear message parents need to get across.

Brian and Delia agreed to run away together. Brian told her not to pack anything; he would get her everything she needed. He also told her not to bring her cell phone so her parents wouldn't be able to contact or track her. He drove to her house in the middle of the night and they left together.

The possible outcomes of this scenario are too horrific to contemplate. Brian, unbeknownst to Delia, was a registered sex offender who had served time in prison. He made a habit of targeting underage girls online. In the UNH study, researchers found that predators had methodical ways of seeking out potential victims. One offender searched profiles for the word "flirt." Another saw a birthday listed in a girl's profile and sent an electronic birthday card. In Delia's case, she had posted a real photo of herself online and described herself as someone who "just wants to be loved."

When Delia's parents discovered her missing the next morning, they immediately called the police. Because she left her cell phone behind in her room, police were able to obtain Brian's cell number and read the messages he and Delia had exchanged. Using information gleaned from the phone, they put together an all points bulletin to law enforcement along the route they suspected the couple would take. The next day, Brian and Delia were located at a gas station across the state line.

Although she had agreed to go with Brian, once she left home, Delia knew she had made a mistake. In person, Brian was not as kind or harmless as he had seemed online. She had gone off with a complete stranger and nobody knew where they were. When the police found them, Delia was so relieved she burst into tears. Although her parents were angry, they were also clearly concerned for her welfare. To help her have a full picture of who Brian really was, Delia's mother asked a police officer to share some of Brian's background. Delia realized that the person she had once considered her true love was nothing more than a criminal.

The fact that kids willingly meet up with people who are out to hurt them makes our job both easier and harder. It's easier in the sense that we don't have to worry as much about random stranger abductions, which do happen, but nowhere near as frequently as we imagine. It's harder in the sense that a lot comes down to parenting. We have to keep lines of communication open so that our children feel we are on their side, rather than enemy combatants.

When it comes to online predators, kids need to understand why these relationships are inappropriate and often damaging. Adults who seek out minors online, whether it's through gaming or chat rooms or other means, do not have good intentions. Of that we can be sure. They may or may not disguise their identities. In many cases, they will be open about their motives. They may say outright that they are looking for a sexual relationship.

We can and should teach our kids to be wary about giving out personal information and engaging with strangers online, but we also need to consider the fact that some kids are doing so anyway. These kids, who may seek attention, have family problems, be socially awkward, curious, or bored—all common conditions in the teen years—are already prone to making bad decisions. The key is to have the kind of parent-child relationship where you take an interest in your kid's life, know what he or she is up to, and are available and willing to talk in a way that at least appears to be accepting and non-judgmental.

Delia's experience left her with scars that will heal

but never disappear. She regrets her actions, but cannot do anything to change what happened. "He acted like he cared about me, but he didn't. He was only out to get what he wanted. I knew that it wasn't right. I knew he was too old. But he just seemed so perfect. That should have been my warning, because nobody's perfect. I learned the hard way, but I'll never do anything like that again."

If we don't want our children to learn the hard way, we need to equip them with the resources to make the right choices and the confidence that we're here for them in case they need help making those choices.

4
CHECK YOURSELF: INAPPROPRIATE MESSAGES AND PHOTOS

When Josh, a boy she had admired from afar for years showed an interest in her, Millie was thrilled. At 16, she had little experience with dating, and thought that Josh was "so cute." Josh, a senior on the football team, spent a lot of his free time at practice, but the two began texting often.

"It was just silly stuff, about school and the team and our parents, how boring this teacher was or how annoying or whatever. He loved to joke around."

At times, Josh's texts took on a romantic tone. "He would tell me how beautiful I was, how he missed me. He asked me to send him a photo to keep on his phone, so I did. It was just a goofy selfie. He sent me one of himself too."

One night as the two were texting as usual before

bedtime, they began to play a game of virtual truth or dare. "We went back and forth with the truth questions and then I picked dare. Josh dared me to take off my shirt. So I did. Then he said, 'How do I know you really did it? Send me a picture.' And that's how it started."

In all, Millie sent Josh five photos of herself in various states of undress, along with what she described as "flirty messages." He was ecstatic.

"It was exciting when I sent them. He promised to delete the pictures. I trusted him. I never imagined he would do what he did."

Instead of deleting them, Josh shared the photos with teammates, who forwarded them on to other students. The compromising pictures spread like wildfire. "A friend of mine called me in the morning and told me she'd seen the photos. She said everyone had seen them. By the end of that day, they were on the website."

The website in question featured Millie's photos, along with similarly risqué snapshots of other high school girls, under the heading "Easy Street." The language used to describe the girls was crude and cruel. The site accused them of being promiscuous and claimed to be doing the world a favor by "outing" them. Under Millie's photo was the caption, "Good girl gone bad." Also included were some of the messages she had sent to Josh. Millie was devastated.

"I didn't want to show my face at school," she says. "I couldn't understand why Josh had done something so mean. I thought he cared about me."

In the end, Millie did go to school and endured the humiliating taunts and snickers of her classmates. Worried that her parents would find out, she decided to tell them herself. "They were mad, but worse than that, they were disappointed and sad. I really felt like I'd let them down. And they were furious with Josh too. They called his parents."

You have probably heard of sexting, or sending sexually explicit messages or images via cell phone or over the Internet. These communications can be forwarded, as well as uploaded to one or more of the many sites available for sharing photos and videos. Sometimes there is an element of coercion or pressure involved, as in Millie's case. She wanted to impress and please Josh. In other cases, the child or teen might send the image or message unprompted.

Items of a sexual nature are not the only form of inappropriate content teens share. Images and messages that are racist, homophobic, misogynistic, violent or just plain malicious are of course equally inappropriate. But because sexual posts and posts featuring R-rated content comprise a significant portion of the communications between teens, and because they often lead to problems, they deserve their own spotlight. For the purposes of this chapter, I am talking about photos, texts, and messages that minors take or write themselves. This differs from images taken illicitly by predators through webcams or hidden cameras, which fall into the area covered in Chapter 3.

According to a survey by The National Campaign to Prevent Teen and Unplanned Pregnancy and CosmoGirl.com, 20 percent of teens aged 13 to 19 sent and/or posted nude or seminude pictures or video of themselves. The figure was only slightly higher for girls than boys (22 versus 18 percent). Even more teens, 39 percent, said they had sent sexually suggestive messages.

Adolescence has always been a time when kids test their independence. The teen years are when they do the things they don't want parents to know about, whether it's smoking a cigarette, breaking curfew, or simply disobeying a parental instruction. This behavior is all part of being a teenager. This is also the time in their lives when they are discovering and exploring their sexuality. They are curious about their bodies. The difference now is that there are ways to explore that curiosity via technology. And because the teen years are also when judgment is not at its sharpest, they can use technology to share highly personal thoughts and images without regard for the consequences, which in this day and age can be very serious.

Millie's experience speaks to one of the main problems with sexting or any kind of inappropriate posting: unintended audience. When she sent her private texts to Josh, she meant them for his eyes only. Instead, they ended up the viewing pleasure of her entire school and untold numbers of strangers.

Kids should ask themselves if this text, message, or photo is something they would be happy for the whole school to see? If the answer is a resounding no, then they should take the finger off the "send" button and instead click "delete."

The second major problem has to do with the permanence of cyberspace and our virtual footprint. Emmett, a graduating senior, was looking forward to graduation. He had applied early to college and was accepted at his first choice, a small liberal arts school in the Northeast. With his immediate future secured, he went about enjoying his last semester of high school. During spring break, he attended a party held at the vacation home of a friend. Emmett, like others at the party, indulged heavily in alcohol and ended up in the pool sans clothes. Although he remembered little the next day, he was surprised to find photos of it on his Facebook page. He had been tagged in several memorable shots, including one where his pants were hanging around his ankles and the name of his future college was written in marker across his bare bottom, along with a choice expletive. Other unflattering photos followed. Emmett untagged himself and asked the poster to remove the photos from the site. Unbeknownst to him, Facebook was not the only place the photos existed. Six weeks later, shortly before graduation, Emmett received a letter from his dream college. The offer of admission had been rescinded.

A 2013 Kaplan Test Prep survey of college admissions officers found that 29 percent Googled an applicant and 31 percent checked Facebook or other social networking sites to look up prospective students. When doing so, 30 percent reported that they found something that negatively impacted an applicant's chances of being accepted. It should come as no surprise that colleges are using technology to find out more about their applicants; many employers do the same with their prospective hires. Some enterprising students try to remove all personal trace of themselves on the web, deactivating accounts, setting up profiles with false names, deleting photos, and trying to erase all potentially incriminating evidence. But even if teenagers remove all the questionable material they know of, there is no way to guarantee that others have not stored it elsewhere, making it potentially accessible to a search.

A communication sent from one device to another feels direct and private, but the truth is that it can be forwarded, copied, and shared ad infinitum. And technology that claims to protect our privacy can add to the problem. Take the example of Snapchat, a mobile messaging app. The app is supposed to allow users to send photos for a one-time only viewing. The sender specifies how long the photo should remain active. The idea is that when the time is up, the photo disappears forever from the recipient's device. Think back to the self-destructing message in *Mission: Impossible*. As it turns out, Snapchat did no such thing. Indeed, as the Federal Trade Commission outlined in its case against Snapchat, there were several ways to save the photos and videos indefinitely, including via third party apps and simple screen grabs.

Servers can be hacked. People can take screenshots, download images, and save messages. The bottom line is that whatever your kids put online should be considered permanent and public. Once they hit the "send" or "okay" button, the photo has left their control and is now floating perpetually in cyberspace.

In previous generations, including mine, when parents talked about protecting our reputation and preserving our integrity, they were talking chiefly about behavior, with a particular emphasis on how we behaved when we were in the public eye. While we might not always have behaved impeccably, for the average person, there was no sense that our bad behavior would be recorded and made public. That was something that happened to celebrities. Now, every teenager with a cell phone can play the role of paparazzo. Everything can be and is recorded for posterity: every drink, every party, every indiscretion, every racial slur or sexist comment.

Kids need to know and understand that cyberspace is not their living room. It feels familiar and comfortable and they are happy to hang out there all day, sending and receiving. And because it feels as cozy as their living room, they find themselves doing things that should probably only be confined to their actual living room. It is up to us as parents to point out that in this environment of constant connectivity, anything you say or do can be used against you.

Millie's parents were angry and disappointed when they found out the details of what had happened to their daughter. But telling them was the best thing

Millie could have done in a bad situation. They took action immediately, contacting Josh's parents and the school. In doing so, they were able to keep the situation from escalating further, although all involved quickly learned that there were serious ramifications to their actions.

Sexual images of a minor are considered child pornography; taking such a photo or forwarding it can lead to arrest. Teenagers have been charged and sentenced for taking and transmitting photos of a sexual nature, even if the photos were of themselves. Law enforcement officials have some leeway in determining whether charges should be brought. In Millie's case, the police decided not to file charges. Josh and some of his teammates, who had been responsible for the malicious website, were removed from the football team and suspended. Millie, while facing no formal punishment, nevertheless suffered. Her image as a hardworking, well-behaved student was tarnished forever.

Most parents think their kids are good kids. Millie is a good kid. Emmett is a good kid. They both made foolish decisions. Believe it or not, your kids are capable of making foolish decisions too, which is why you need to talk to them. Have a discussion about what kind of communications are acceptable to send and receive electronically. It's important to note that this is not just about inappropriate sending. If your kids are on the receiving end of anything questionable, they should let you know immediately. Be open about it. Ask to see their phones. There shouldn't be anything on there that they are unable to show you. This doesn't mean there won't be silliness; they are kids, after all. But anything that crosses the line into suggestive or sexual or R-rated territory should raise a red flag.

If you are not comfortable talking about topics of sexuality, you need to find a trusted adult who is, because ignoring it isn't going to make it go away. Why wouldn't you want to prepare your child for the next stage of his or her development? You can't opt out of being a parent, and preparing your child for the realities of life is part of being a good parent.

This may sound like a lot for kids to think about, and it is. I once had a parent tell me, "My parents used to say, 'Don't do anything I wouldn't do.' But nowadays, it's not just about doing something stupid. It's, 'Don't do anything I wouldn't do, but if you do, please don't let it wind up on YouTube!'"

Emmett remembers lots of people taking photos the night of the party. He even took some himself. Remind your children that they are in control of their lives, and by extension, of the way they are perceived. They can't assume that their friends and acquaintances are going to make the best decisions on their behalf. This is the same logic we apply to drunk driving. We teach our kids not to drink and drive, but beyond that, we teach them not to get in a car with a driver who has been drinking. Good judgment includes avoiding those who do not exercise it.

Make sure your kids know that they can always come to you with their problems. Tell them that you will love them always. If they do confide in you, give them the reassurance that they've done the right thing in doing so. Don't add to their distress by lashing out. This is not to say that you shouldn't be angry; anger is a natural reaction. But you also need to be able to focus on finding a solution to the problem and providing support to your kid. From birth, children look to their parents to help alleviate pain and make things better. Your first response may be, "What were you thinking?" Your next response should be, "What is done is done. How can we fix this?"

For parents who grew up in the pre-Internet age, it is difficult to imagine just how much technology is a part of our children's lives. Tell them that there were no computers when you were a kid, and they will be truly shocked. It is not possible to shield them from the devices of the modern age. You've probably seen a toddler navigate an iPad with the ease of a NASCAR driver behind the wheel. They intuitively know how it works. They get it.

What they don't get, and Millie is a good example, is where it can lead. If life is like a chess game, you as a parent are thinking several moves ahead in advance. You know what the pitfalls are; you can see what lies on the path ahead. Kids, on the other hand, are firmly stuck in the present. Millie admits that she never imagined the images she sent in a moment of recklessness would be used to humiliate her and tarnish her reputation. She was operating completely on impulse, not instinct. But teenagers are not without the capacity for reflection.

Once, when my own child was little, we were at the store and she saw a little boy standing up precariously in a grocery cart. She looked down at the seat belt fastened over her lap and asked, "Why can't I stand up like him?" I looked over at the boy and replied, "Is that a good idea?" She thought about it. "No," she said. "Why not?" I asked.

"Because he could fall down," was her answer. Even at that early age, she could figure it out, given a few extra seconds.

If we teach our kids to take those few extra moments to consider before they send, hopefully they too will come to the right conclusion. In my presentation to kids, I advise them to "Think before you click." They might just as easily ask themselves, "Is this a good idea?"

When his college offer was rescinded shortly before graduation, Emmett was at a loss. The future he'd dreamed of for so long now seemed impossible. His parents sat him down to discuss his options. All agreed that college was still the goal, but it would have to wait another year while he reapplied to schools. In the meantime, he could find a job and live at home.

As Emmett began filling out college applications for the second time, he decided to use his online experience as the basis for his personal essay. His parents thought it was a risky move, but he insisted. The admissions people were likely to find out about it anyway, he said, so it was better to be open about his mistake. The essay he wrote was frank, honest, and remorseful, but also resilient. His gamble paid off. Emmett received offers of admission from three colleges.

5
SECURE THE PERIMETER: THE PASSWORD PROBLEM

Mike, a suburban father of two, had worked as a regional sales manager for a major cell phone company for seven years when he was called into his supervisor's office for a closed-door meeting.

"I could tell it was serious because we would usually joke around a little before getting down to business, but this time there was none of that," says Mike.

His boss Rajesh cut to the chase. He had received several complaints from Mike's co-workers about his comments on Facebook. Mike was mystified. He had a Facebook account, but hardly ever posted anything. He used it mainly to keep in touch with old school friends and relatives.

"Of course I told him I had no idea what he was

talking about, because I really didn't. His reaction was that I might as well admit it, because the evidence was there for everyone to see."

What evidence, Mike wondered.

An increasingly annoyed Rajesh pulled up Facebook on his desktop computer and turned the monitor around. On the screen was Mike's personal page, with several status updates underneath his profile photo. As he began to read them, he was filled with a growing dread. Each update was a line or two of virulently racist, sexist, or homophobic text.

"I was speechless for a second," remembers Mike. "And then I blurted out something like, 'I didn't write that,' which sounded exactly like something a guilty person would say."

There was more. Rajesh said it was bad enough that Mike had posted offensive comments on his own Facebook page, but what made his conduct worse was that he had also posted similar remarks on the company's public Facebook page. Those had been deleted, but Rajesh had saved a screen capture and shared it with a horrified Mike.

"It felt unreal."

As it turned out, his boss had not just called Mike in for a reprimand. Citing the company's strict policy against racial harassment and the need to maintain a tolerant work environment that embraced diversity, Rajesh informed Mike that they could no longer keep him.

Stunned, Mike returned home to tell his wife Julia. As the couple contemplated how to break the news to their kids, many questions remained unanswered. "I couldn't believe it was legal for my company to let me go like that. Wasn't I owed some due process? What happened to innocent until proven guilty?"

But more than that, husband and wife were mystified at how the hostile remarks could have appeared on his Facebook profile. Although some of his Facebook friends were co-workers, Mike was almost certain he had never visited the site at work.

"We tried to think of it logically. Was this someone who was out to get me? Well, he or she would need to be able to get into my Facebook account. Who knows my password?"

Passwords are an inescapable part of modern life. We use them to access everything from our kids' grades to email, banking, and online retailers. Many sites are now requiring ever more complex passwords that include both upper and lower case letters, symbols, and numbers. You may have seen that feature where websites rate the strength of your password as you are creating it. No one wants a "weak" rating. But even as passwords become more complicated, they must also continue to be memorable. Most of us have had the experience of resetting our password. Some people reset their password on a regular basis because they cannot for the life of them remember what it is.

In addressing the password issue, we are talking about both your passwords and your children's. As soon as our kids enter elementary school and begin to use their own passwords, they need to understand how to safeguard them. At the same time, chances are they also know the access code for your phone or mobile device, and, as they get older, the password for your home network and other accounts.

In February 2012, news emerged that the email accounts of several senior Syrian government officials, including the president, had been hacked and hundreds of emails leaked. Upon further investigation, it turned out that many of the accounts had the same password: 12345. This was the default password, which nobody had thought to change. According to password management company SplashData, which compiles an annual list of the top 25 worst (aka most frequently used) passwords, 123456 happens to be the most common password in usage. Here is the entire top 10 list for last year:

123456
password
12345678
qwerty
abc123
123456789
111111
1234567
iloveyou
adobe123

If you're currently using any of these, now's the

time to change passwords! The trick is to choose something that is easy enough for you to remember, but difficult enough to withstand guessing. To achieve this balance, it's best to avoid choosing a random assortment of letters and numbers that you will have no hope of recalling. Similarly, you don't want to use something as obvious as your pet's name.

No matter what method you employ to come up with your password, be sure to avoid some common pitfalls. Don't include any identifying numbers in your password, such as date of birth, age, address, or phone number. Do not use your own name, or the name of anyone in your immediate family, or geographic locations that are easily associated with you.

I have an effective method for choosing passwords that I like to share with my audiences. Choose a song you're very familiar with, something you know the words to, and take the first letter of each word in the first line. For example, the Beatles song "Yesterday" begins with the line, "Yesterday, all my troubles seemed so far away." As a password, that would be YAMTSSFA. Many sites require you to use a password that includes a number and/or symbol. Using a number one for the letter I, or a zero for the letter O has become quite common, so you should steer clear of that pattern. Try using a three for the letter C, since it's the third letter of the alphabet, or use the symbol above that number on the keyboard. The important thing is that it is a system that you can remember.

I recommend having at least three different

passwords: one for your email account, one for your banking and other finances, and one for everything else. Change them every six months or so. You can choose three songs by the same artist, but it means you only need to remember three songs at any one time. The number of passwords your kids need will depend on their age and the extent of their online activity. Younger children will likely only need one; teenagers may need two or three. The nice thing about the song lyric method is that every child knows a few songs that they can easily bring to mind.

Mike racked his brain, trying to imagine who could have accessed his account. "The Facebook password is the same password I use for my email account and the same password I use for the wireless network. And we're going through this list of places where I use the password and a terrible thought enters my head. The kids. The kids know my password."

Once Mike's thoughts turned to his kids, he felt an urgent need to question them. While Julia couldn't imagine either of their sons capable of doing something so vicious to their father, she agreed that kids can be prone to bad judgment and thought maybe a friend had put one or both of them up to it.

They sat the boys down, told them that Mike had lost his job, and explained the reason why. Carter, 16, and Cameron, 14 were understandably confused. Mike said he believed someone had played a prank on him without realizing how serious it was. Now they needed to figure out how it had happened. As he spoke, he tried to gauge their reactions. They were both visibly upset, but there was no immediate confession of wrongdoing.

"I asked them if they knew anything about it. Both boys said no. Then Julia said that whoever had posted the messages had to have my password. And the only people who knew that password were the four of us, unless they knew differently. Again, they had no information. Julia and I believed them. So that seemed to be a dead end."

The first step in securing your online presence is to create a strong password. The second is to keep it a secret. It doesn't matter how impenetrable your password is. If you share it with someone, it might as well be 123456. Telling someone includes writing it down or putting it on a post-it note and leaving it lying around. It may seem like a no-brainer to keep your password to yourself, but password sharing is a common occurrence.

In a study commissioned by the Family Online Safety Institute, 34 percent of teens said they have shared one of their usernames and passwords with someone other than their parent or guardian, including 23 percent who have shared it with a friend or significant other. This happens for a variety of reasons. Sharing a password is viewed as a symbol of friendship in the digital age. For those in a romantic relationship, it represents trust, demonstrating that neither partner has anything to hide from the other. There are also practical reasons for sharing passwords. If one person has paid for something that offers exclusive access, such as Netflix, or a site that plays music, sharing passwords enables multiple people to benefit from a single subscription.

From the moment your child starts using a password, make it clear that he or she must not share the password with anyone. Some law enforcement officials tell parents that they should know their kids' passwords so they are able to keep an eye on their online interactions. This is a personal decision for each parent. If you have an open and honest relationship with your child, then hopefully this will not be necessary because you'll have access whenever you ask for it.

If you do not have a computer in your home and regularly use public computers, such as at a school or a library, go through the safety precautions with your kids. Tell them to check and make sure other people are not watching as they log on. Make sure they sign out of their email accounts completely before leaving the computer. If given the option, do not allow the computer to remember the password for future use. And because they are in a place where strangers congregate, kids should never allow anyone else to get on the computer they are using while they are logged in.

Sharing passwords applies to YOUR passwords as well. Again, whether or not you give your passwords to your children is up to you, but ask yourself this: do they really need to know? What is the upside? If they need your password to purchase an app or complete some other online activity, isn't it better that they have to come to you?

The day after Mike and Julia spoke to their sons, the younger one, Cameron, sought out his dad.

"He wanted to know if there was a date on the Facebook posts, so I gave him the date. I asked why. He said he had been going over it in his mind and he thought he might be responsible for what happened."

Mike gently asked Cameron if he had written the posts. His son's denial was immediate and vehement. No, it wasn't him, but he thought he knew who might have done it.

Zach and Cameron met in preschool. Growing up in the same neighborhood, they were in and out of each other's houses throughout childhood. By the time they reached middle school, they were no longer close friends, but still saw one another now and then. On the day of the Facebook posts, Zach had come over to hang out while contractors worked on his house. Cameron, who had a science fair project due the next day, was too busy to be social. Zach didn't seem to mind. He had his phone to keep him occupied, but didn't want to eat into his limited data plan. Could Cameron give him the password to the home network? He could and did.

At the end of his story, Cameron broke down in tears, feeling guilty about his dad's predicament.

"I told him that he wasn't responsible for Zach's actions, if Zach was the one who had done this. And anyway, I've given out the wireless password to guests on more than one occasion myself. The important thing was that this was a lead, and I was going to follow up on it."

Mike started with Zach's parents, whom he knew well. They were dismayed at the suggestion that their son had done anything wrong, but allowed him to talk to Zach in their presence. When Mike first mentioned the Facebook posts, Zach's immediate reaction was also vehement denial, but when he heard about Mike losing his job and the permanent repercussions, he grew quiet and remorseful. He admitted logging into Mike's Facebook account—without premeditation, just out of boredom. Cameron had left the room to work on his project in the kitchen. Zach got onto Cameron's desktop and went to Facebook. He was curious to see if the network password worked there too. When he was able to sign on, it was exciting. He navigated through Mike's page and his friend's pages incognito.

But why the malicious posts?

"There wasn't a satisfactory explanation for that. Zach said he was just messing around and intended to delete the posts immediately, but then Cameron came in, so he quickly logged out. And the posts stayed up."

With this new information, Mike went back to his employer to explain what had happened. Zach's parents backed up his story. Rajesh was sympathetic. Mike was reinstated in his job, but not for long. Despite the clarification, the atmosphere at work had changed. It no longer felt welcoming to Mike.

Colleagues were courteous, but kept their distance, as if they couldn't quite let go of their suspicions about him. After a few months, Mike left of his own accord.

Peer pressure can make it difficult for kids to refuse when friends ask for their password. Be sure and tell your children that they can use you as an excuse not to give it out. They can make you the bad guy and tell their friends that Mom or Dad won't allow it, or that they'll get in trouble at home if they do. Practice the scenario with them so they know what to say and aren't put on the spot if the situation arises.

Passwords can be a very effective security measure if used properly. Hackers, con artists, and data thieves value passwords precisely because they are conduits to valuable information. Like a skeleton key that opens any lock, a single email password can unlock many doors. To prevent that from happening, we have to be responsible password users. If kindergarteners are old enough to have passwords, they are old enough to understand how to protect them and why. Even as adults, we need constant reminding. As Mike came to understand, there is no age limit on vigilance.

Mike does not blame his son for what happened. After all, he admitted to doing the same thing himself. But the lesson learned came at a high price. "Passwords are such a part of our lives that we don't even think about what they represent," he says. "It's easy to think of them as the equivalent of telephone numbers, especially when you're talking about a network password. But they're much more than that. They're the key to our identities, our wallets, our employment, and our security. Once that perimeter is breached, a lot of damage can be done."

6
PLAY IT STRAIGHT: ILLEGAL DOWNLOADS AND FILE SHARING

Ethan is a big *Dr. Who* fan and has amassed an impressive collection of memorabilia from the English television series. When a friend told him about a site where he could download every *Dr. Who* episode ever shown on TV, Ethan was skeptical at first. Then he visited the site. It blew his mind.

"I felt like a kid in the candy store. I asked my friend if he was sure it was all right to download the shows. He said he did it all the time. Even his father did it. He had downloaded all the Disney princess movies for his little sister."

Excited, Ethan began downloading *Dr. Who* episodes onto his family's desktop computer. Sites like the one Ethan used are known as "torrent" sites, named for the technology they employ to break down and transmit the files.

If the story ended there, Ethan would still have a big problem. Illegally downloading copyrighted material is against the law and can lead to criminal and civil charges. Criminal penalties include prison time and fines of up to $250,000. Civil penalties include up to $150,000 per copyright infringement. Remember those piracy warnings that precede the movie on a DVD? They're for real. If you think that these are just scare tactics and not enforceable, think again. In 2012, a federal appeals court upheld a jury's decision to award $675,000 to the Recording Industry Association of America after it sued a teenager for illegally downloading and sharing 30 songs. A mother in Minnesota was fined $1.5 million for the songs she downloaded.

But you don't need to get into copyright law to explain this to your children. The most basic argument against sharing music, movies, and games across computers or over the web is that it is the equivalent of stealing. This is a simple message that even younger kids can grasp. If you didn't pay for it, you can't have it.

On that first day, Ethan downloaded a dozen episodes. The next day, he went back for more. As he explored the site, he saw that there was a lot more available than just old TV shows. The newest movies were there, along with music by all his favorite artists. He spent hours trawling through the inventory.

The desktop computer Ethan used is also the one his parents use for online banking, paying bills, shopping, and other general household tasks. A few days after Ethan started downloading, his dad Javier got on the computer to check his bank account. He was shocked to see that the primary checking account balance was $2,000 less than it should have been. Looking through the transactions, he saw that the amount had been transferred out of the account the day before. Thinking that maybe his wife had made a large purchase on the joint account without informing him, Javier called her at work to inquire. She had no idea what he was talking about.

Next he called the bank. The banking agent told Javier that the money had been transferred through his online portal, meaning that whoever did it needed his user name and password to log in. She noted that it was a joint account and asked if Javier had checked with the co-owner. He had, and neither he nor his wife had shared the login information with anyone else. The agent asked if the computer was in a public area or accessible to others. No, replied Javier. The computer was in the den, and the kids used it occasionally, but it wasn't available to outsiders. He went through the process of reporting a fraudulent transaction and cancelling their debit cards. As advised, Javier and his wife also immediately changed their login information.

While the incident was disconcerting, Javier was satisfied with the bank's response and resolved to put it behind him. Then, just days later, his email account was hacked. Friends contacted Javier to say they'd received suspicious messages from his address. Finally, another unauthorized withdrawal appeared on the checking account. The bank's fraud department again questioned the security of his computer.

At a loss, Javier asked his brother-in-law Andy, an IT specialist, to come in and look at the desktop. Andy did a thorough check of the hard drive and had bad news for Javier. He located the episodes of *Dr. Who* and with them, files that contained malware, or malicious software, designed to infect the computer. It appeared to Andy that this particular malware contained a keystroke-logging program that transmitted keystrokes back to its home base. In other words, someone somewhere was able to track all the information typed on the keyboard, including user names, passwords, account numbers, and more. That was how they had managed to get into Javier's email and crack his banking password not once, but twice.

When Javier asked Ethan about the files he'd downloaded, Ethan didn't understand how TV shows could have caused the problems his dad described. Javier explained how viruses and other forms of malware are embedded in files that may look normal, but are in fact designed to spread throughout a computer and execute malicious acts. He likened them to an illness. You don't see the germs passing from one person to another, but several days later, when the symptoms hit, you know you've been infected. It was an analogy that resonated with Ethan.

From a young age, kids learn how to keep from spreading germs by washing their hands, not sharing drinks with friends, and covering their mouths when they cough or sneeze. These simple tips are useful in preventing the spread of disease and developing good hygiene habits, but are equally applicable to staying safe online. Just as bodily viruses can harm you physically, virtual viruses can be destructive financially and emotionally and leave you vulnerable to future attack. An easy first step is to make sure your antivirus software is up to date and run virus scans regularly. Show your kids what you're doing and explain why. It's a hand washing for the computer!

Inform your kids that it's in their interest to keep the computer clean. In addition to the fact that there are penalties for piracy, there's also the fact that by inadvertently downloading a malicious file, they can mess up the computer or device. Tell them that if anything goes wrong with the machine and the damage is due to illegally downloaded files, you won't get it fixed or they won't be able to use it any more.

When I was growing up in the 80s, we also shared media, but we did it via the mixtape, a compilation of songs recorded from various albums onto a cassette tape. If we wanted to share a TV show, we had to use a VCR. And when we copied albums, we were only passing along music, not our parents' bank account details and Social Security numbers.

If the illegality and potential danger don't dissuade you, consider the environment. If you have never visited a torrent site, you may imagine it as a slightly less legitimate Netflix. In fact, it's more like an online version of a black market adult video store. Visiting one is similar to entering an unfamiliar and sketchy neighborhood. You start to see strip clubs, stores with bars on the windows, people loitering, and derelict buildings. It's the same when you're on a dodgy site. It doesn't feel right because it's not right.

These sites make their money from advertising, and what is a guaranteed moneymaker in cyberspace? Pornography. If your child is on a torrent site, you can be sure he or she is seeing lots of ads for porn sites. It's also the kind of place where lots of bad things are lurking—viruses, spyware, malware—as well as potentially unsavory people. At the very least, they're lawbreakers for downloading. They could also be much worse. All in all, it's not a wholesome environment for a kid, especially when the Internet offers so many child-friendly places to hang out.

Kids today are used to instant gratification. If they want to see a TV show, it's on demand. If they want to view the latest music video, there's YouTube. Just about everything they could ever want is available online for purchasing, viewing, or downloading. The key is to teach them that just because something is available, it doesn't mean that they can or should have it.

As parents, we don't want to be in the position of always saying "no." Instead, we should say, "do it safely." If you don't want your kids to download illegally or share files, offer them alternatives. If they don't already know, tell them about legal music streaming services such as Spotify, Pandora, and Songza, which offer basic listening services for free. Take them to the public library to browse the DVD and music collections, also free. If they feel as though they need to own the item, they can set aside a portion of their allowance or you can set a budget for the purchase of one item every month, or whatever schedule fits within your means.

Gift cards and prepaid cards are good alternatives to cash. They offer kids the freedom to download apps and media, but set a limit on the amount that can be spent. They are also reloadable and offer peace of mind to parents who are uneasy about giving kids access to adult credit cards.

With Andy's help, Javier was able to get the malware removed from his computer. The *Dr. Who* episodes were also deleted. Ethan was given strict instructions never to download anything without permission, and banned from returning to any torrent sites.

As computer users, it's impossible to avoid sharing or downloading files. We all do it from time to time, whether we're working on a project with others, buying an app, or updating software. As with everything related to the web, it is important to be cautious in doing so. Remember that in cyberspace, things are not always as they seem. A file with an innocent-sounding name can be pornography. An app for a kid's game can contain a nasty virus. When you do purchase apps, go directly to your service provider's approved vendor to buy them. If you are buying apps for your kids' use, turn off in-app purchases, so they will not be in inundated with offers. Turn off the ads. Give your kids an online experience that that is as controlled as it can be. Software updates should come from the device or software manufacturer, not a third party. Pop-up screens are notorious for being conduits to viruses. Disable them through your browser's settings. If you are not computer savvy, get a knowledgeable friend or relative to help.

A little careful consideration goes a long way. Tara, a high school junior, was preparing to take her Advanced Placement Chemistry exam. A group of students from her class created an online site to share notes and tips, post questions, and plan study dates. It was a useful resource and gradually expanded to include students from other schools.

"At first, it was just a few kids that I knew," says Tara. "And then it grew. It started off with posting our notes from class and labs. If there was something I didn't understand or needed help with, I would post a question and someone would answer it. There were common files we could access—handouts from the teacher, practice tests, things like that. But as more people joined, it started to go off on a tangent. There were people I didn't know, and they started posting things that had nothing to do with chemistry at all."

One of Tara's classmates, Sung Hee, tried to get things back on track. "She sent out a message that was basically a plea to focus on the AP exam, which was coming up soon. It seemed to work for a while. Then one day, someone whose name I didn't recognize posted that he had a copy of the actual exam, and he would share it with us. Well, the place went nuts. Some kids objected, saying that we would all get in trouble if anyone found out. Other kids wanted to see it. There were some people who didn't believe him and thought it was all a prank. "

Tara was one of those who tended toward disbelief. "There were a lot of things about it that seemed fishy to me. The chances of it being the real test were very slim as far as I could tell. Where would he even get it? But if it was the real thing, I didn't want to see it, because I'm not a cheater. If it wasn't the real thing, what was the point of sharing it? But most importantly, who was this guy? I considered it a Pandora's Box. I didn't see any good that could come from opening it. So I didn't."

Several of her fellow students did, however, including Sung Hee, who insisted that she'd had no intention of cheating, but was just so curious she couldn't resist.

"I texted Sung Hee later that day to see if she'd opened the file. There was no reply. Then a while later, I got a frantic phone call from her. She said that all the files on her computer were corrupted. All her reports, projects, homework, college applications, everything was fried."

Sung Hee was not alone. Other classmates who downloaded the exam file had similar reports of files damaged and data lost. The document in question did have test questions on it, but they appeared to be sample questions available freely on the web.

"They tried to track down the original poster, but they never could find out who it was, and we never heard anything more from him. We weren't sure if he even was a student, or someone who had snuck in. That worried us, because we all shared personal information and if he was someone with bad intent, who knows what he could do with it? Sung Hee and the others lost a ton of valuable documents and files. They spent a lot of time and effort trying to reconstruct them. We decided to shut down the sharing site to avoid any more problems. And our test prep was shot. Sung Hee ended up not even taking the exam."

Before the dawn of the Internet, our choices were more circumscribed. Things took more time. If we wanted to do research for a paper, we had to go to the library, look through the card catalog (the one with drawers and notecards), locate the book on the shelf, and find the pertinent information. That same process would now take a matter of seconds and could be accomplished without leaving home or even the room. Our kids, having grown up in this environment, are used to acting quickly.

It is up to us to teach them how to pause and think about what they are doing. There are very few instances online that require immediate action and in almost every case, as with Tara, hesitation can be beneficial. I tell kids to "think before you click," but sometimes they need help. Ethan received assurances from his friend that what he was doing was okay, but if he had asked his father, would he have received the same answer?

The ground rules Javier set for his son's computer

use came a little too late. If they had agreed on guidelines from the outset, they might have avoided trouble. We instruct our kids on usage of virtually every other machine, from the stove to the television, but their confidence on the computer can make us think they know what to do when they really don't. Again, focus on the right way to do things rather than just what they're doing wrong.

It should go without saying that if you are telling your kids not to download illegally, you should practice what you preach. Be a good example for them. When they get to college, they will find that each school has explicit policies regulating copyright infringement and codes of conduct governing computer use on the college's network. By then, students should be well-practiced and responsible digital citizens.

Tara attributes her caution to a natural skepticism, but says that there were warning signs too. "There are almost always warnings signs," she says, "if you know what to look for. If anything is out of the ordinary or doesn't make sense, it's a tipoff. If you buy milk at the store, it will be milk. But no one's regulating the Internet. Even the news can be fake. So we have to regulate ourselves."

As for Ethan, he is still a *Dr. Who* fan, but now looks to add to his collection via Ebay and used bookstores.

7
TALK IT OUT: OPEN COMMUNICATION

There is a sexting case brewing in Virginia that provides useful insight into why it is important to engage your kids early and often on the subject of online behavior. The case involves a teenage couple. The girl is 15 and her boyfriend is 17. The girl sent her boyfriend photos of herself and in return, he sent a sexually explicit video. The girl's mother intercepted the video and filed a complaint with police. Police arrested the boy and charged him with two felonies: possessing and manufacturing child pornography. For this, he faces jail time, as well as lifetime inclusion on the state's sex offender registry.

Whatever your opinion of the merits of this case, the fact remains that teenagers often make unwise decisions. In fact, they're known for it. In this case, both girl and boy are guilty of questionable judgment, but the boy's lack of forethought could land him in jail. These actions can have serious consequences.

If there is a recurring theme in this book, it's the need for communication. I do not claim to be a parenting guru, but I do understand kids, and I know that it's good to talk. Our modern lifestyle makes it easy to avoid conversations with our children, but we do so at our own peril, and theirs.

The Internet is an amazing tool with unbelievable benefits. You can chat with family and friends for free and find educational resources, information, and entertainment instantaneously. Social media has sparked revolutions around the globe and allowed us to follow unfolding world events in real time. Our children can watch videos on YouTube that teach them how to play the guitar or make crafts. It is no exaggeration to say they have the knowledge of the ages at their fingertips. But the very qualities that make the web so attractive are the same ones that make it equally dangerous. It is accessible, universal, and anonymous.

People can access the Internet from the farthest reaches of the planet. You can just as easily connect with someone online on the other side of the world as you can someone in the next room. It is universally available and understood. And it is anonymous. There is no immediate way to verify someone's identity. If you're in the same room as someone who looks 50 and claims to be 15, that lie is easy to spot. If your archenemy Mandy comes up to you claiming to be your best friend Ella, you know it's not true. You have all working senses at your disposal to help distinguish between a lie and the truth. When that information comes to you in a series of typed words, you are at a severe disadvantage. You can take a chance or play it safe.

In life, in the real, physical world, we sometimes take what we call a calculated risk. That means that we weigh up the pros and cons, the possible pitfalls and benefits, of an action. If it looks like we have a decent chance of success and the downside is not too damaging, we go for it. Online, because we don't have all the information, we can't make the proper calculations, so we should always play it safe.

In every horror movie, there is a moment when one character heads off to confront certain death. As viewers, we always wonder why someone would do something so foolish. It's almost as if they have no idea what the consequences might be. It's the same with our kids and technology. When they act foolishly, it's because they're living in the moment. Like the doomed characters in the horror films, they my not even know what the possible consequences are. It's not sufficient just to tell them what might happen. We need them to internalize it. So, ask them. What are the possible outcomes if you send an inappropriate photo to someone? What could happen if you make fun of someone online? This requires them to think, to speak, and to take an active role rather than just be a passive listener. This is the process you want them to go through when they have their finger poised over the send button.

Hopefully, most of the interactions our kids have online are harmless and can be carried out without fear of consequences or repercussions. But some online activity should give them pause. If we can teach our kids to build in an extra 20 seconds to think things through before they act, they would likely be able to avoid the riskier behaviors. This is the whole premise behind the message, "Think before you click."

National Public Radio's Diane Rehm recently hosted a show on the subject of human trafficking. One of her guests was Bill Woolf, a detective with the Fairfax County Police in Virginia. Detective Woolf pointed out that technology has been an asset to traffickers, who can learn a lot about kids from the Internet and can use it to reach a large number of people at once. A father of four daughters called in to ask what he could do to keep his kids safe. The detective responded, "I would say the most important thing is to be involved in your daughter's lives."

Be involved in your children's lives. This may seem obvious, but let's think about how much time we spend engaging with our kids. This is different from simply being with our kids, because as we all know, we can be in the same room or car with our kids without having anything to do with them. We've all seen the sad sight of families out to dinner, each person on his or her own device. These days, an entire family can be watching TV in the same room without even watching the same show. We have cars with separate entertainment units for the front and back seats. Because of our busy lifestyles, fewer families sit down to meals together. How many times have you seen a child eating a meal in a car? Maybe even in your own car? I had a mother tell me that she went into school to have lunch with her daughter and after a while she found herself looking at her watch because she was not used to sitting still and talking to her daughter face-to-face for so long.

The first thing we can do as adults is set a good example and put down our own devices. We hardly know what to do with ourselves if we are not looking at our phones or tablets. Remember the viral video of the woman who was so engrossed in texting that she fell headfirst into a mall fountain? Disengaging from technology has to be more than an intention. We must schedule technology-free time. You could make it a household rule that no one is allowed to use an electronic device during dinner, or set aside some time in the evening or on the weekend when you get together as a family to play a board or card game. Take regular walks together. If you're fortunate enough to live in a city with good parks and recreational facilities, check them out. Americans are very good at scheduling activities *for* our children, but not as good about scheduling activities *with* our children.

If you are reading this and your immediate response is, "I don't have time," let me stop you there. Lack of time is not an acceptable excuse. Sure, we're busy. All you have to do is drive on the highway at rush hour to see that the pace of modern life is hectic. It is easy to become fragmented and distracted by the competing pressures on our time and attention. Juggling professional and personal commitments requires organization and concentration. We have come to believe, with the aid of technology, that we can and must do more. We are accustomed to instant messaging, 24-hour supermarkets, microwave ovens, and drive-through dry cleaners. But nothing has changed. There are as many hours in the day now as there have ever been. Assigning a sense of urgency to every single task leads to frustration and inefficiency. Take time instead to prioritize. And your first priority should be your children.

Once you have designated time without electronics, talk to them. Ask your kids about their friends, how things are going at school. Ask them if there is anything bothering them or any other kids at school. What are their hopes and dreams? What are their fears? Do you know what their current favorites are? What music are they listening to? Do they know any good jokes? I talk to kids all the time, and I can tell you that they are fascinating conversationalists, if you give them a chance. Don't underestimate them. You may not realize what's on their minds, but if you give them a chance, they'll tell you.

Find out how they are using technology. Familiarize yourself with what's considered the norm at your kid's school. Does everyone have a cell phone? A smartphone? Does anyone use email or is it all texting? Share with them the guidelines provided in this book. Tell them some of the stories. Give them an open invitation to chat with you anytime they feel uneasy about something they encounter online or are unsure what to do. In school, when they are teaching emergency procedures, they present the kids with scenarios. What do you do if a fire starts in your house? Where do you go? This way, children have concrete steps to take should the worst happen. Do the same when you're talking to your kids about technology. What do you do if you get a message from a stranger? What if someone you met online wants to meet in person? Who should you tell if you receive a nasty message from a schoolmate?

There are many unknowns in the virtual world, and as adults, that makes us fearful. Our kids have their own fears. Childhood and adolescence can be an unsettling time. They look to us for stability and guidance, and we need to instill in them a sense of confidence. Kids need to know that however uncertain things may seem, they are always in control of their own minds and actions. They should trust their instincts. We do not expect our children to be perfect all the time, but if something feels wrong to them, it probably is.

Erin, the mother from chapter one, blamed herself for her daughter's bullying behavior. She was not the only one.

"I know the parents of the bullied girls thought we were bad parents. How else could our daughter turn out to be a bully? Obviously we had done something wrong. I believed it myself and spent a long time feeling depressed about that. I finally realized, with the help of counseling, that there was nothing I could do to change the past, but there was a lot I could do to keep it from happening again."

Erin had a head start on the parents of some

bullies, who refuse to acknowledge their kids' wrongdoing and remain in denial. She set about trying to repair the relationships within her family.

"When the girls were little, we used to play with them a lot more, even if it was just pretend tea parties with the teddy bears. As they grew and became more self-sufficient, they were able to occupy themselves. In a way, it's a relief that you don't have to spend as much concentrated time watching them, entertaining them."

Erin initiated a weekly family game of Scrabble and forced her warring daughters to compete together as a team. All mobile devices had to be shut off and put in a basket out of sight.

"At first the girls were resistant and they argued even as teammates, but after a while they got into the spirit of it. Teaming up against their parents was probably even more fulfilling than taking on each other. We knew things were going well when they began high-fiving each other every time they came out with a high-scoring word. It brought the tension level in the house way down."

Erin also resolved to spend one-on-one time with each daughter. When Nina began taking a yoga class, Erin tagged along. She brought her sewing machine down from the attic and enlisted Ashley's help in making a quilt. The increased togetherness led to more conversation, and most importantly for Erin, more opportunities for listening.

"I felt suddenly as though all these years had gone by. They were under my roof and I saw them every day, but I'd lost track of them somehow. I had to get to know them again."

Erin expended a lot of time and effort to get her family back on track, and her determination paid off. Her story illustrates how to make the best of a bad situation, but we'd all rather avoid the bad situation to begin with.

There is no way to get around the spread of technology, nor should we want to. Even if you are not buying your child a mobile device, your school district may be. An increasing number of schools across the country are supplying their students with tablets for use at school and at home. In 2013, the Los Angeles Unified School District announced a plan to give each student an iPad. When they put the plan into action, however, it immediately ran into problems. Within days of receiving their iPads, many students had learned how to hack into the system to remove security filters installed on the devices. A year later, the distribution is on hiatus as the district explores other options, including the purchase of laptops.

It appears that in some cases, the development of technology may be outpacing our ability to get a complete handle on it. This is particularly true for large institutions, but something we can also relate to on an individual level. We just get the hang of our operating system when a new one comes along. We love the way our phone works and then we have to replace it. Google Maps is awesome, and then it improves and some of our favorite functions are impossible to find.

The end result is that we bestow this technology on our children without preparing them adequately. Think about it. We would never consider giving a car to a teenager without teaching the kid to drive, making sure he or she passed both a written exam and driving test, insuring the car, insisting on seat belt usage, and delivering several lectures on the importance of safe driving. Yet we're quite happy to hand a child an iPad. For a seven-year-old, an iPad is the technological equivalent of a sports car. It looks great, and you can drive it, fast, anywhere you want to go. No lessons, no test, no license, no lectures. Just charge it up and away you go.

Part of the reason that parents sometimes fail to teach their kids the proper use of technology is that they themselves are not that familiar with it. They may not have grown up in the virtual age. Technology may intimidate them. Or they may not understand the dangers it can pose.

The purpose of this book is to show parents, educators, and other responsible adults that you do not need to be an expert in technology to understand the risks. Similarly, you do not need to install expensive and complicated software to protect your children. We can go a long way toward keeping them and ourselves safe just by adopting the common sense approach I call CyberSense. I keep my slogan brief and memorable because even if our kids don't remember every detail of what you (or I) tell them, they will remember this: Think before you click!

APPENDIX A

DISCUSSION QUESTIONS

I've included a list of questions that can be used as a starting point for conversations with your children about online safety. Remember that these interactions should be discussions, not interrogations. The questions are intended to stimulate discussion, so feel free to adapt them to your own individual circumstances and invite your child to ask questions as well.

1   Be Nice: Bullies in Cyberspace

Have you learned anything at school about cyberbullying? What is it?

Has anyone ever said mean things to or about you

online?

Have you ever seen general trash talk online?

Is anyone you know experiencing online harassment?

Have you ever sent a message that said something mean about someone?

How do you tell the difference between teasing and bullying?

What would you do if someone was bullying you online or if you saw someone else being bullied?

2   Keep it Under Wraps: Identity Theft and Privacy

What kind of information is considered personal identifying information? (Examples include name, address, phone numbers, birth date, age, Social Security number, drivers license number, schedule, and school name and grade.)

Do you ever put your personal information online? What kind of information and where do you post it?

Do you know who can see it?

Is there any personal information that shouldn't be shared with the public?

What do you think people could do with your

personal information?

Do you know what identity theft is? How can you prevent it?

3   Don't Engage: Avoiding Online Predators

Do you know what the privacy settings are on your social media accounts? Let's make sure your personal photos and information are kept private.

Have you ever received a communication (text, email, phone call, etc.) from a stranger? Or played a game with someone you've never met?

Have you ever written or spoken to a stranger online?

How can you verify someone's identity when you're on a computer or a mobile device?

Has someone you met online ever asked to meet you in person?

What would you do if someone did ask to meet up with you?

4   Check Yourself: Inappropriate Messages and Photos

What kinds of messages and photos do you consider

inappropriate?

What would you do if a friend asked you to send something inappropriate? What would you do if he or she sent you something inappropriate?

What are the dangers of sending inappropriate messages and photos to other people? What could happen?

Do you know anyone who's done anything like this? What happened?

5   Secure the Perimeter: The Password Problem

Do you have more than one password? How many do you have?

How do you remember them?

Do you ever change your passwords?

Have you ever shared your password with anyone? Who? Why did you share it?

Can sharing passwords create problems? What kind of problems?

What's the best way to protect your passwords?

6   Play it Straight: Illegal Downloads and File Sharing

Do you know what illegal downloads are? What kind of things can you download?

Where do you go to download files?

Why is it illegal?

Do you share files on your computer with other people online? How do you do it?

Are there any dangers with file sharing or illegal downloads?

What are the safer alternatives to illegal downloading?

7   Talk it Out: Open Communication

Have you ever felt uncomfortable while you were online, either with something you saw or something someone said?

What did you do about it?

Do you ever feel stressed about how people behave online? Do you feel pressured to act a certain way?

Do you feel like you always have to check your phone to see what's going on? What happens if you don't?

Do you feel like there are any rules about how people communicate electronically? Should there be?

Are things that happen online that adults know nothing about? Are they things that we should know about?

Would you feel comfortable coming to me if something was bothering you? Have you ever wanted to talk to me about something but felt like you couldn't?

APPENDIX B

RESOURCES

American Academy of Pediatrics (AAP)
http://safetynet.aap.org
This site provides links and resources from the AAP and other organizations that specialize in keeping children and adolescents safer online.

Common Sense Media
https://www.commonsensemedia.org
Common Sense Media publishes independent ratings and reviews for books, movies, TV shows, apps, and games so parents can determine what material is age-appropriate for their children.

CyberSense Program
http://www.cybersense-program.com
Find information on how to bring James Munton's

exciting assembly program to your school. Watch videos and read reviews.

Federal Trade Commission (FTC)
The FTC is the nation's consumer protection agency. The site contains detailed information about identity theft and protecting kids online.

> Identity Theft
> http://www.ftc.gov/idtheft

> Kids' Online Safety
> http://www.consumer.ftc.gov/topics/kids-online-safety

Microsoft Safety & Security Center
http://www.microsoft.com/security

National Center for Missing & Exploited Children (NCMEC)
This is the leading nonprofit organization in the U.S. working with law enforcement, families and the professionals who serve them on issues related to missing and sexually exploited children.

> http://www.netsmartz.org
> Netsmartz is the NCMEC's interactive, educational program offering age-appropriate resources to help teach children how to be safer. The program is designed for children ages 5-17, parents and guardians, educators, and law enforcement.

http://www.nsteens.org
This NCMEC site is designed for tweens and teens.

Pew Research Center's Internet & American Life Project
http://www.pewinternet.org
The Pew Center conducts surveys that examine how Americans use the Internet and how their activities affect their lives.

Stop Bullying
http://www.stopbullying.gov/cyberbullying
The federal government's anti-bullying site Stopbullying.gov has a dedicated section on cyberbullying.

Webonauts Internet Academy
http://pbskids.org/webonauts
The PBS Webonauts Internet Academy is an interactive online game for kids aged 8-10 that teaches them how to be good digital citizens. Also included are tips for parents and educators.

ABOUT THE AUTHOR

James Munton is a national speaker and author on the subjects of online safety, deception and identity theft. His school assembly programs receive the highest praise from educators, students and parents. *CyberSense: Think Before You Click!* is his popular program for middle and high school audiences.

James has appeared on ABC, NBC and Fox News and has been featured in articles in The Washington Post, The Wall Street Journal, The Dallas Morning News and Woman's World magazine. James has performed at the White House three times.

While other children played soccer in the park, James spent his formative years in the company of London's cardsharpers learning how to be a card "mechanic." A local magician steered his talents in a more honest direction and, following an apprenticeship in the art of legerdemain, James began performing magic professionally in 1993.

After graduating from university, James taught at schools in England and Japan while developing his entertainment business. Since moving to the United States in 1997, James has provided educational entertainment to hundreds of thousands of students.

James has made a lifelong study of scams and cons. His first book *The Con: How Scams Work, Why You're Vulnerable and How to Protect Yourself* was published by Rowman & Littlefield. As a national speaker on the subject, James helps individuals and organizations keep their personal information secure. In response to the huge problem of child identity theft, James created a program for middle and high school students. He realized that cyberbullying, sexting and online predators all have a common link: young people are sharing too much information online, often without thinking of the dire consequences.

CyberSense: Think Before You Click! is a 45-minute assembly program that teaches children about online risks and then presents them with easily implemented solutions to protect themselves.

For more information, call 1-888-773-2155 or visit http://www.jamesmunton.com

17682585R00065

Printed in Great Britain
by Amazon